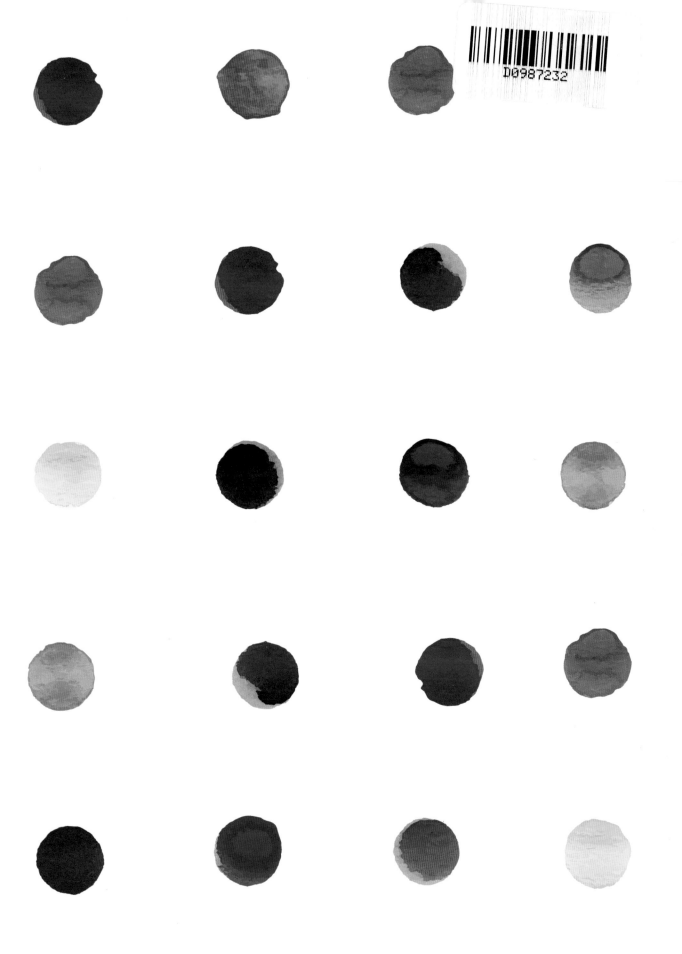

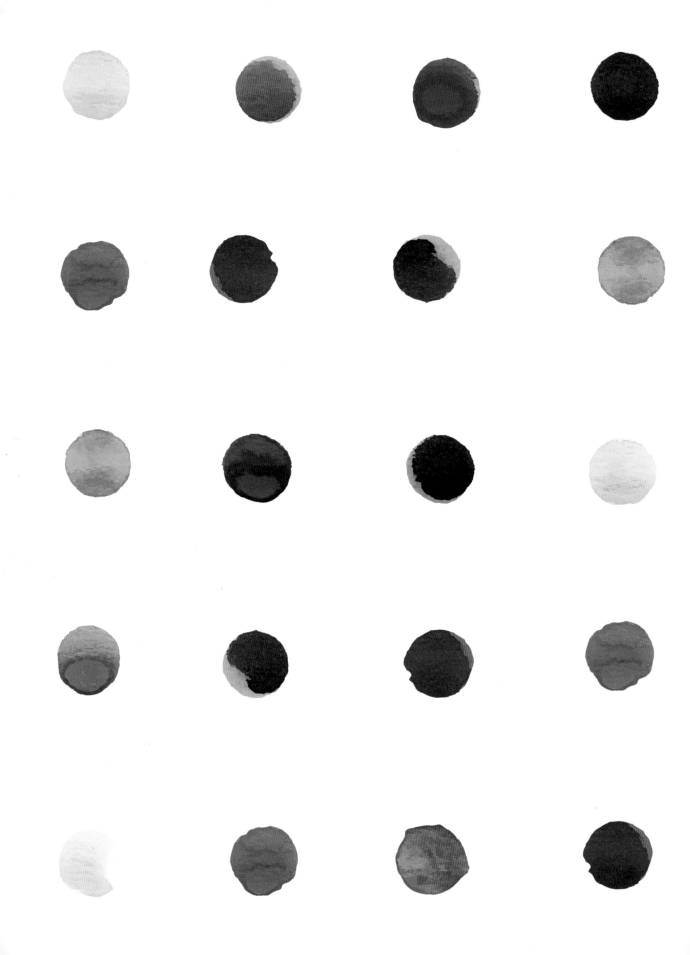

This book is dedicated to my family for their love, patience, and sense of humor.

www.mascotbooks.com

Fantastic Features of Peculiar Creatures

For more information, please contact:
Mascot Books
620 Herndon Parkway #320
Herndon, VA 20170
info@mascotbooks.com

CPSIA Code: PRT0319A
ISBN-13: 978-1-64307-415-3

Library of Congress Control Number: 2019901276

Printed in the United States

FANTASTIC FEATURES
OF
PECULIAR CREATURES

Amy Solaro

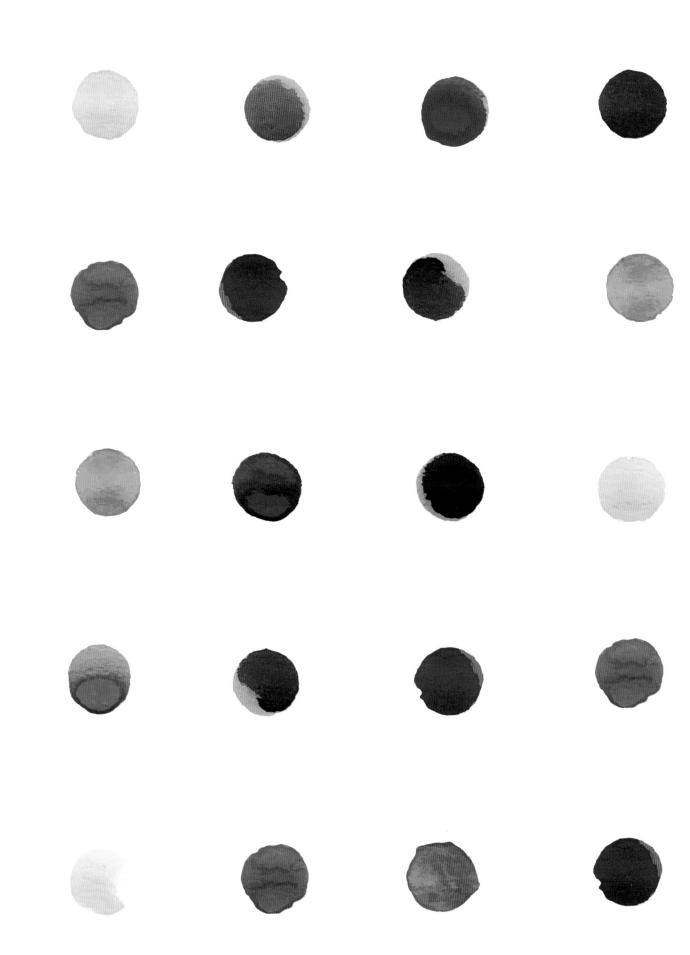

Hello! We're animals from around the globe
Here to have our stories told!
Though rarely considered cuddly or cute,
These poems will make such issues moot.
There's more to us than how we look
As you'll see as you read this book.

THE DUNG BEETLE

D to the U to the N to the G!
Dung beetle is the name for me!
P to the O to the O to the P.
I eat poop exclusively!

With more than 8,000 different species,
You'll find us anywhere there's feces.
We're strong and mighty and so great!
We can lift 50 times our body weight!

We're also excellent recyclers,
Disposing of what's found in diapers.
By burying and eating dung,
We're eco-heroes, oft unsung.

Our consumption helps improve the soil,
Dispersing seeds with our toil.
Because we dispose of livestock waste,
We make this world a cleaner place.

So now you see our role is key.
Dung beetles help everybody!

THE VULTURE

Soaring in circles from high above,
We carefully search the ground for grub.
We're scavengers so we eat rotten meat.
It's called carrion and it's our favorite treat!

We delight in many great adaptations
That have evolved over generations.
Our strong stomach acids protect from disease,
And our nearly bald heads make clean up a breeze!

We know that many think it's gross
And wouldn't attend a dinner we host,
But with our A+ vision and razor-edged beaks,
We think we are pretty neat!

We're a crucial part of our planet's web,
Cleaning up leftovers and preventing germ spread.
Think of us as garbage trucks
Getting rid of all the yuck!

THE VAMPIRE BAT

When day becomes night and the sun hides its light,
From an upside-down slumber, I stir.
With super-duper smell and sight,
My soaring's so quick it's a blur.

First of all, I must confess,
Blood is the meal that I like best.
But please don't be afraid of me
For humans aren't my cup of tea.

I prefer four-legged creatures
And those with avian features.
Pigs and cows and horses, too,
Birds that caw or squawk or coo.

Heat-seeking nerves in my wrinkly face
Allow me to swoop in on meals with grace.
We're social creatures with families and crews
Living in caves from Mexico to Peru.

We share our food with one another,
Generous to our moms, dads, and brothers.
So, if south is where your travels take you,
We hope we get to see you too!

THE TARANTULA

Very hairy and oh-so scary...
That's what people think of me.
But it's not true, I say to you
For my venom's weaker than a bee!

With hundreds of types in our family tree,
We live in many different places
From desert sands to tropical seas.
We dig burrows, not webs, for our living spaces.

We hunt at night using our legs and bite,
Pouncing on mice, frogs, and bugs.
Our fangs inject venom that is just right
To dissolve a meal we can chug.

Our regeneration super power is really very cool—
We shed our exoskeletons in order to expand,
And we regrow legs and organs, too—
Very useful during our 30-year lifespan!

So, when you think of giant spiders,
please don't let out a screech!
We're a key part of the animal kingdom
and are amazingly unique.

THE STAR-NOSED MOLE

Have you ever seen a creature with a star on its nose?
A small hairy rodent that digs tunnels with its toes?
You guessed it! It's a star-nosed mole—the star of this poem.
Though he seems strange at first, try getting to know 'em!

His tentacled nose forms a 22-arm star—
With 100,000 nerve fibers, super sensitive they are!
This makes their sense of touch incredibly equipped,
With five times more nerves than your hand in one fingertip!

Besides his name-sake nose, he has another claim to fame.
He's the world's fastest eater, putting challengers to shame!
One quarter of a second—just the blink of an eye—
Is all it takes for him to swallow worms inching by.

His expansive tunnels provide oxygen to plants near and far,
So, don't be grossed out by his nose—this guy is a star!

THE PROBOSCIS MONKEY

Honk, honk, roar!
Who's that down by the shore?
Don't worry, it's just me—
a proboscis monkey!

I only live in Borneo,
Eating leaves and tree roots as they grow.
This menu makes my belly round
And creates symphonic farting sounds.

Named for my gigantic nose,
I rarely inspire romantic prose.
Though not a honker most would pick,
It helps me make my loud music.

Because of webbing on my feet
I'd beat most swimmers at a meet.
I love the water, love to swim,
Love to belly-flop from a mangrove limb.

Honk, honk, wheeee!
Proboscis monkey—that's me!

THE BLOBFISH

Blobbity, blobbity, blobbity blue,
I'm from down under; how about you?
Living on the seafloor of the ocean is intense,
It's down so far that the pressure is quite dense,
To scientists I'm mostly a mystery,
I live so deep that it's hard for them to see!

I'm boneless and flabby
with colors quite drabby.
No muscles nor teeth,
I live deep underneath.
Though I wobble like jello
I'm a handsome fellow!

Squishity, squishity, squishity squish,
It's me—the lovable blobfish!

THE SLUG

I'm slippery, slimy, but not at all grimy.
I live in your garden, leaving trails slick and shiny.

My slime is a major multitasker
And helps protect me from disaster.
It coats sharp objects over which I roam
And its chemical blend maps my journey home.

I have two pairs of tentacles on my face:
One for my eyes, one for touch and taste.
I can retract them when I feel shy,
But be patient and soon I'll pop out to say hi!

I turn rotten plant matter into my food,
So please don't squish me—that'd be rude!
Take a good look at my cute little mug,
I'm just a little garden slug!

WHERE WE LIVE

VULTURE

VAMPIRE BAT

STAR-NOSED MOLE

TARANTULA

LIVE EVERYWHERE BUT ANTARCTICA:
- SLUGS
- DUNG BEETLES

PROBOSCIS MONKEY

TARANTULA

VULTURE

BLOBFISH

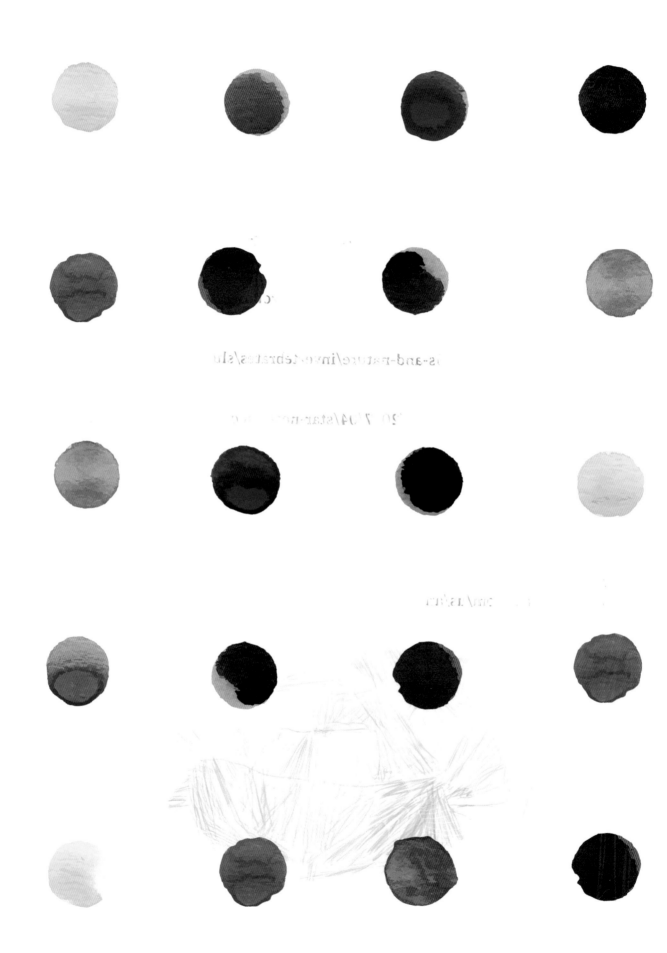

Where to Learn More:

Blobfish
animalsake.com/facts-about-blobfish-ugliest-fish-in-ocean

Dung Beetle
natgeokids.com/uk/discover/animals/insects/dung-beetle-facts

Proboscis Monkey
nationalgeographic.com/animals/mammals/p/proboscis-monkey

Slug
dkfindout.com/us/animals-and-nature/invertebrates/slugs-and-snails

Star-Nosed Mole
news.nationalgeographic.com/2017/04/star-nosed-mole-touch-pain-senses

Tarantula
kids.nationalgeographic.com/animals/tarantula/#tarantula-closeup-hand

Vampire Bat
kids.nationalgeographic.com/animals/vampire-bat/#yikes-vampirebat

Vulture
www.dkfindout.com/us/animals-and-nature/birds/vultures

Coloring Pages

Coloring Pages

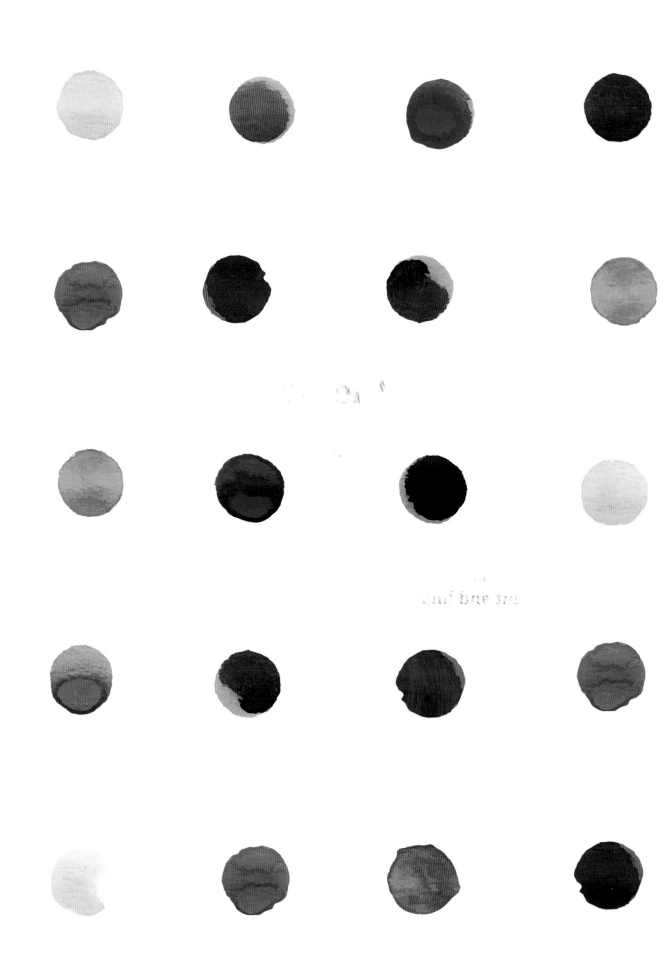

About the Author

Amy Solaro is an artist and children's book author. She was raised in Reno, Nevada, and spent her young adulthood in Los Angeles and San Francisco. She currently resides in Columbus, Ohio, with her husband, two young sons, their dog, Pete, and two goldfish. Her inspiration for writing comes from the irreverent and hilarious minds of her two children.

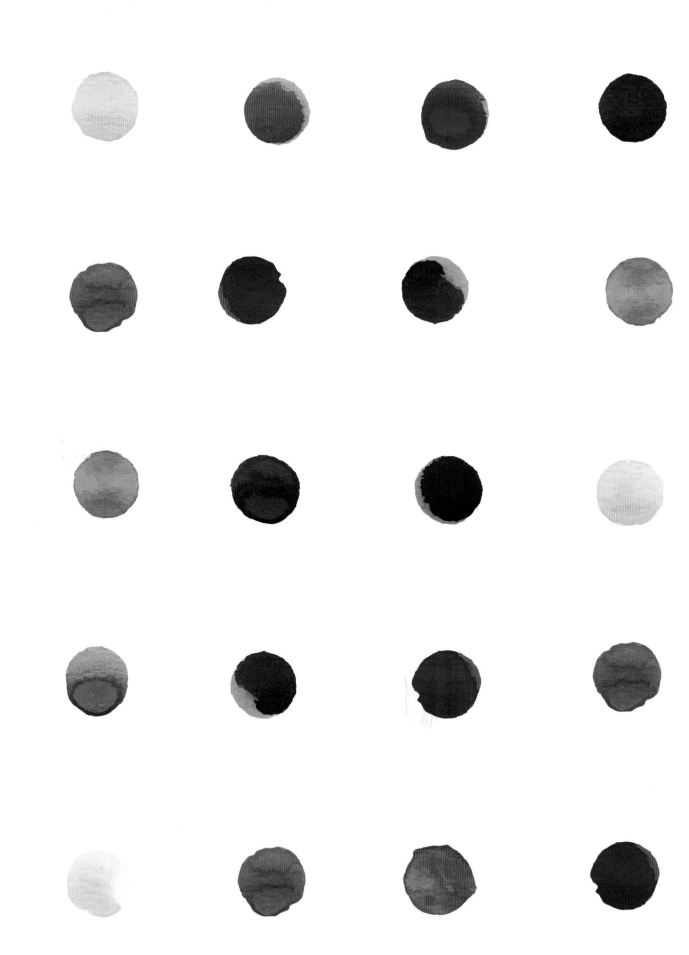

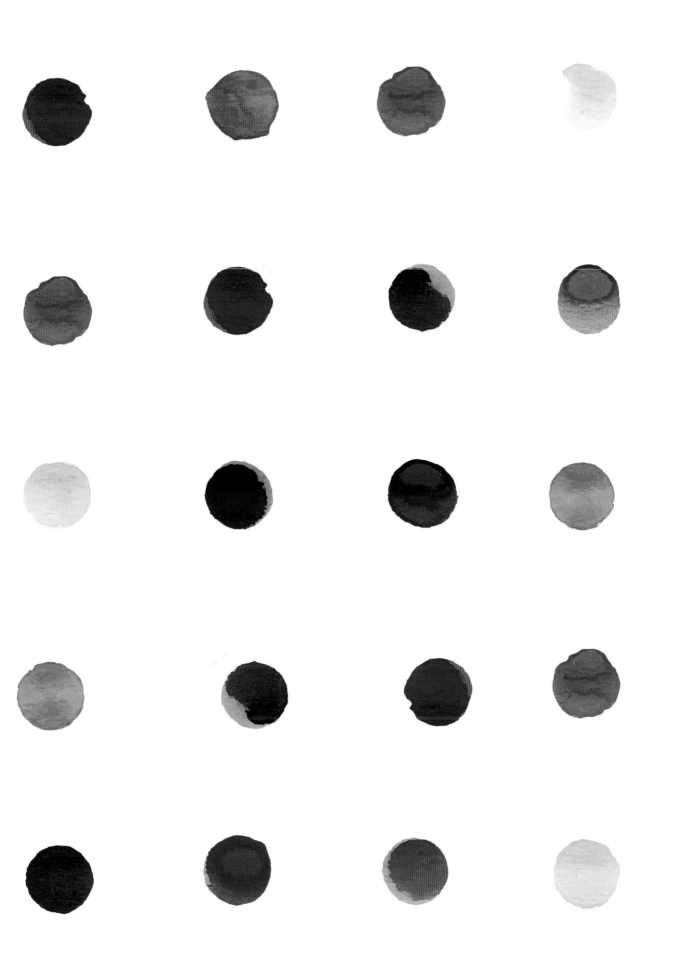

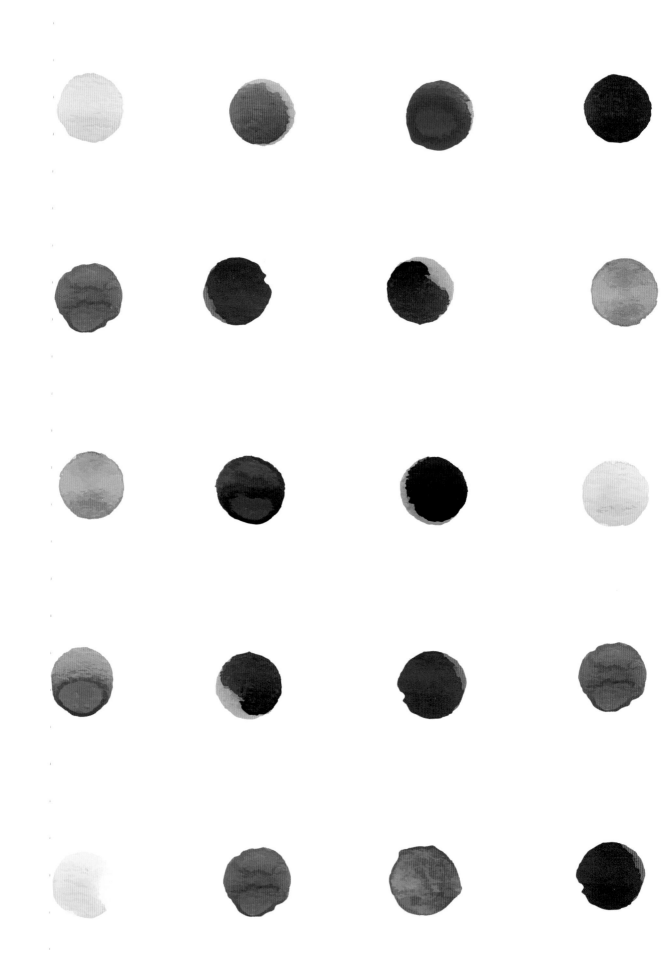

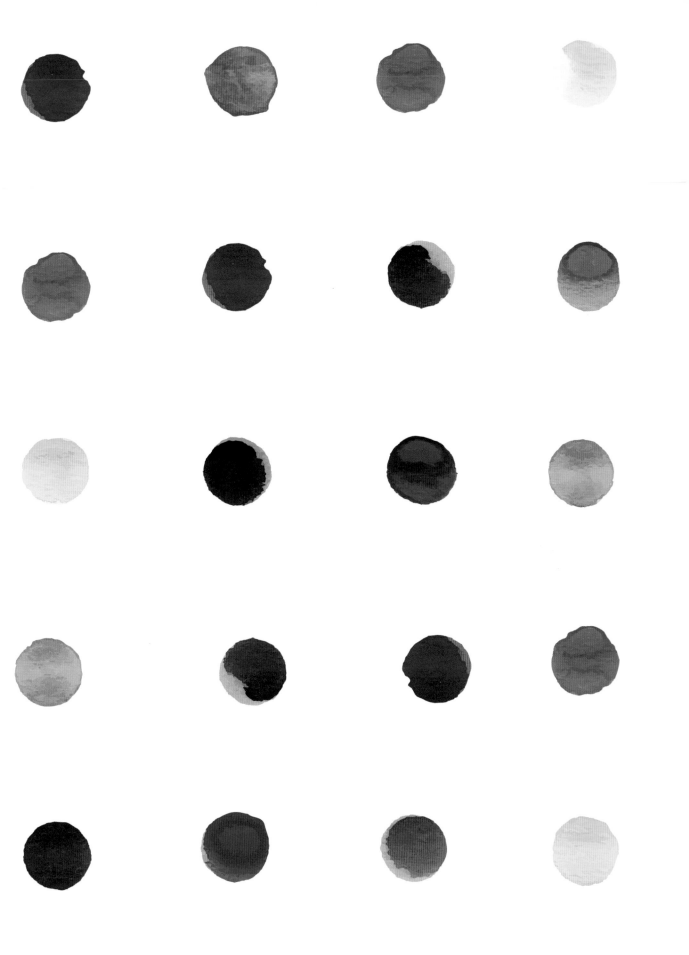

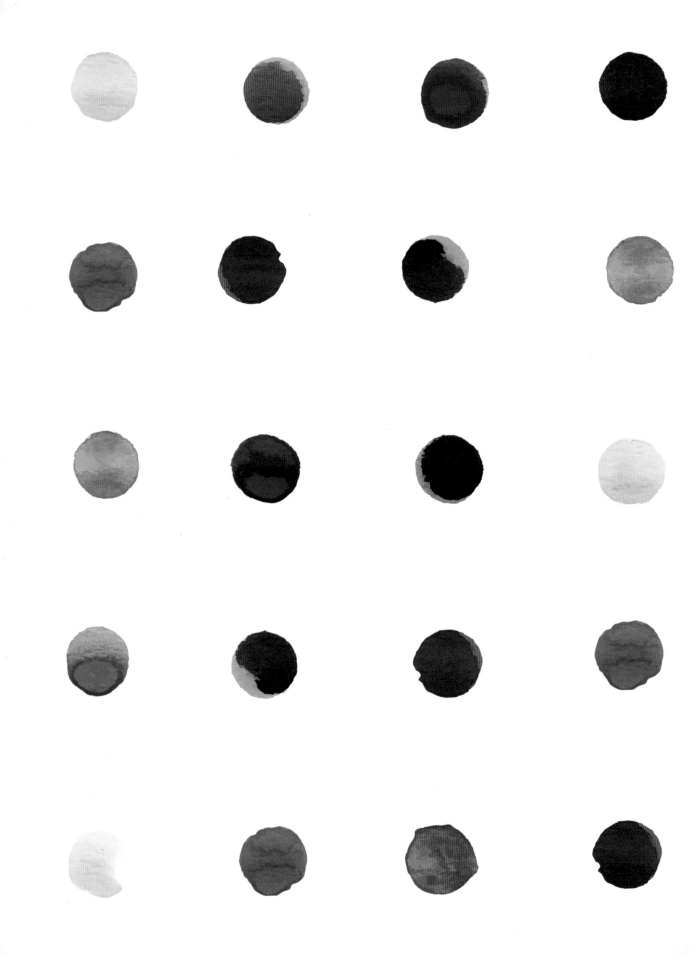